MW00785437

To Deidre

" Wishing you gentle healing "

all my love,

Eliza
Limmy

Copyright © 2020 by Alejandra Jimenez
ISBN: 978-1-7361496-0-7
Published by Alegria publishing

All right reserved. No portion of this book may be reproduced, with the exception of short quotations and reviews, without permission from the author or publisher as permitted by U.S. copyright law.

Cover/ Book Design by Sirenas Creative | Diane Castaneda and Omar Castaneda
Cover Illustration by Veronica Sotelo
Portraits by Corina Villegas & Jasmine Romero
Author Photo by Alejandra Jimenez

Mujer de Color(es)

Alejandra Jimenez

Shadow Work

Rebirth

Contents

"You may call me
A gitana, a hippie, a flower child, a wild woman, a serpiente, a bruja
With grace,
I will wear these labels as a badges of honor
If it means that I am a woman free to choose
Her own path,
Chant her own songs of life,
And be true to her soul's calling."

- Aleja

Preface

Dear Reader,

I had longed for a place to belong to for so long. Feeling alienated, like
the other: for my brown skin, for being a Mujer, for being a lesbiana, for
being a desdichada, for being the daughter of immigrants, for being too
promiscuous, for not being promiscuous enough, for believing there is
a God, for not believing in the right one. This place of soledad, left me
voiceless time after time. It confined me deep inside my thoughts, in and
out of reality, between my feelings and the sheets of paper that laid in front
of me. In that dark place, words began to form on paper. Many of those
words were not mine but projections from the outside world. What others
thought I was. What others expected me to be. But finally, buried deep
beneath, my own voice began to make its way to the surface. I discovered
poetry. The beauty, the ugliness, entangled with one another. I felt things
very deeply, at times I felt things in the place of others. Often more deeply
than they felt it themselves. A masoquista is what my Ama called me. "Nos
gusta la mala vida," were the words of amor she gave to me. It was her way
of telling me, I had inherited a bloodline of copendency, a formula for
sorrow and pain, from my mother's mother to her and from her mother's
mother before her. She said it with a charismatic tone of submission. As if
we should accept the traditions that harm us, that quiet us, that erase us.
My words are for you ama, abuela, tia, amiga, vecina. Que estas palabras
nos sirvan como una voz para protestar aquello que nos silencia y reclamar
aquello que nos libera.

Con todo mi ser,

Aleja Jimenez

For my Ama, my Macorina, my hermanas, my tias, my abuelas, my mentors, my ancestors, and for you.

Gracias for being the source of my strength and motivation when I could not find it in myself.

Shadow Work

Before Blooming

Healing isn't always a blooming process

You must let the water flow

Take its natural course

Allow it to fill you up with sadness

Until the soil begins to move

Showing you the hollow spaces in your soul

Feel the discomfort

Sit with the wetness

The emptiness

With the fear that you might never be whole again

Don't fight it

You can clip and clip

At your brown-dying-tips

Make yourself look green and edgy on the surface

Eventually the same pale spots will reappear

If you don't find the source of your ailment

Sure you'll have aphids to keep you company

Make the pain go away for moments

But soon your colorful essence will begin to fade

Not even the maggots will stay around

When there is nothing left of you to consume

Keep healing

Even when all that is left is a crumbling root

Dig up the rotting dirt that hides

Beneath your surface

Expose your insecurities, hatred, misery, lies, enviousness

You may gag at your own festering scent

But even this stench is proof you are still alive

When you allow yourself to stop

Sit with yourself, your respiration for a moment

The ingredients in your environment become more clear

The ones that lead to your decay

The ones that will aid in your healing

Don't stop

You have washed the rot from your roots

Exposed the hollow spots

Sharpened your edges

It is time to add new soil

Replant the remaining parts of you

Water yourself intentionally, carefully

Stretch into the ground

Let time be the final factor in your time to bloom.

Break the Cycle

I was born again, but it wasn't from a place of love. It was a place of profound pain that had eradicated all former concepts of happiness, of wholeness, of being. I had to recreate the womb that would bring me back to life. I was my own mother, nurturing my soul into an existence of light. Being a woman, I had an advantage. I naturally knew that I would need to be gentle but relentless, as my own mother had been. There were times when all I wanted was to run back into the safety of my oppressor's arms. Time and time again I dreamt myself saying the words "I could forgive you and forget it all. All if only you could protect me from the cold and lonely world. The world that lives inside me and I am so terrified to face." But this heartbreak is not mine alone. It is my mother's and sisters' too. I must break free from these chains, the ones my mother passed to me, and her mother passed to her. I must wake up and heal these deep ancestral wounds. Mujeres are systematically taught that their existence is one inherently guilty. Guilty of sin, immorality, and imposition. So we must understand that the guilt we feel so deeply within us, even when the obvious mistake was not our own is because it is so deeply embedded from one generation to the next. We MUST break these cycles. It begins with ourselves. Acknowledging the self-sabotage we mistook for loyalty. All that pain you feel today can turn out to be your greatest source of inspiration. The thing you needed to finally fight for your own inner peace. That's love. And that's what you have been missing the entire time: amor propio. The funny thing is when you hear something like this, the average girl will be like "woah, that's crazy and extreme. That is not my life. I don't suffer in extremity." Yet, women's greatest situations of oppression go unnoticed. It's the enabling actions that are sly and silent that cause the most harm. The possessive significant other, the controlling religion, the machista father, and the enabling mother. All of these roles hide behind practices of tradition so we accept them as the norm, even excusing them as caring habits. Caring words don't always match their actions. We have an inherent sense of right and wrong, an intuition that tugs at our soul when we are being treated unfairly. Don't ignore this sensation, feeling, knowing. Sometimes because we are conditioned to feel guilt, we ignore it. Saying we are overreacting but what if the action was being perpetrated against your mother, your sister, your best friend? We tend to be more protective of other women we love than ourselves and that is key! We are a small speck of a collective, universal, feminine existence. If you can't find the will to stand up for yourself, do so for HER (the mother, daughter, sister, etc). Every time you stand up for yourself you are reteaching the feminine consciousness how to reclaim its value, honor, respect. Breaking the cycle begins with me. Say it to yourself, "breaking the cycle begins with me."

A Letter to Mejicanos a la Mejicana

Dear elders, *mejicanos a la mejicana*, men and women,

who look like my own father, who remind me of my own mother, y mis abuelos, de pueblos, y ranchos, y ciudades no-tan-liberales. I sit here inhaling, swallowing my own pungent smell, the smell of dirt and sweat after being outside all day trying to find, lose, the motivation to write this letter to you. I sit here in this shack I have made my home, surrounded with paintings of Chavela Vargas, Frida Kahlo, and Maria Felix, records de Jose Jose and Lila Downs too, a La Mejicana, to never forget I come from you. My eyes melting into this screen as I think to myself, how far I am from everything that you are. How strange I may seem to you. I am your daughter, your granddaughter, of your own flesh and blood, but there are so many worlds between us. I wonder if you could be proud instead of mortified by my words. By the truths I want to speak, that go against every tradition you have taught me, beaten into me. Oh how I wish I could free you, unlearn you to learn. Teach you all there is not to know. I want to show you all there is to love about women, their sexuality and force. About their softness, about their ability to nurture, to break chains, all with their voice- because my women are calladitas no more. I want to tell you how much I have grown while sharing my life and my bed with a woman, despite all you had to say about Sodom and Gomorrah. Of the life outside the constraints, the restrictions of a binary world. The multidimensions you could live in, if only you would give yourself permission.

> *You may call me a pervert*
> *Look to me with disdain*
> *But*
> *I will not hide*
> *In this world*
> *We fuck*
> *We love*
> *We cheat*
> *We lie*
> *I say this without cynicism*
> *Towards life*
> *Because in all of this*
> *There is beauty too*

How I wish you could hear me, see me and know I am not that different from you. I too wake up, look at our father sun and give thanks for the blessing of a new day. I too kiss my lover each night, never taking for granted her's or the moon's sacred companionship. I too use my hands for labor and to eat tortillas. Yo también honro y cultivó la tierra donde vivo y duermo.

> *Though I know*
> *Maybe, the day you come to understand*
> *May never come*
> *I know*
> *No, I am not that different at all*
> *and completely different, all the while.*

Kindred Soul Hermanas Coll.

Corina Villegas | September 2020

Frida's Self Portrait with Monkeys, 1943

Frida, kindred spirit, hermana del alma

I often frequent you in my dreams

A jungle, paradise

Just for you, me

And Caimito de Guayabal

Your eyes fixed on me

Revealing their agony

Often overlooked

Distracted by your divine posture

Appearing as

A deity of illness, heartbreak, and death

I recognize the interlaces and twists of your life

That now appear as an ornament

Woven into your hair

And the blood that has spilled over time

Embroidered around your neck and over your heart

Wearing the symbol of Ollin

You tell the world

You have evolved into your creature self

Able to see beyond western senses

You wounded sister

Suffered as only I

A woman like you

Could understand

When the agony reaches me

And the blood begins to spill

Dear Frida,

I fix my eyes on you

You who understands my pain

The illness of my soul

You who holds the secrets

Of how to take hold of the spirits of death

And turn them into a painting of color and vigor

Revelations that could only be reached

When I frequent you in my dreams

Do not shut your eyes nunca nunca

Or turn your gaze from me

Don't take away the portal

That leads me to that jungle, paradise.

Wounded Daughter

I've searched for you in
The trees that sway
That try to hold on to the wind
Uproot themselves
Escape their own nature
Fulfill their longing
To fly with the birds

I've searched for you in
The lonely depths
Of hot moist, dusted air
Passing through spinning fan blades
In a paint-peeled, joists-exposed
Molded room off of 4th

I've searched for you in
The muffled, unfamiliar but real voice
On the other end of
My wife's phone
As she whispered into the mic
"I can't wait to be with you again"

I've searched for you in
The blood tracks on the carpet

Stale now, nearly permanent

That duress memories from

The moments when they were formed

I've searched for you

In the lacrimal gland

As it contracted to give birth

A clear liquid secreted, born

Revealing its pain to the world

I've searched for you in

The crevices of a

Carved wood cross

Disfigured, hollow

Far from its creation

It did not speak back

I've searched for you in

Hypoplastic breasts

Unripe, tart

Too bare to feed

Though salivating, starving

Forced to wean off too soon

Hija del Lechero

You, hija del lechero, inherent nostalgia, empathetic to a fault. You who stands 5 feet tall, skin brown, un color canela, even when you tried to avoid the sun so they would stop calling you prieta. "Negra, negrita, mi prieta favorita." It never bothered you when Apa would say it, he said it as if it was something to love. You almost believed it as a child, couldn't help but notice that everyone followed up "blankita" with a smile. That the light complexion of your sister's skin always made her "la mas bonita." That the boys and girls you crushed on, would pick your amiga of light skin, de ojos verdes, y piernas sin fin, over you, a morenita chaparrita. That your curly and puffy hair was even too much for your Ama's hands to tame. Yanking, pulling, tearing, a brush whack to the head porque no te estabas quieta or was it because no matter how much she brushed no dejabas de ser una greñuda. Hija del lechero they called you. De donde sacaste ese pelo, ese color de piel? No lo heredaste de tu padre, tampoco de tu madre. Has de ser hija del lechero. But that inherent memory of where you came from could never be erased, no matter how hard you tried to suppress it. Blend in with the rest. Your piel canela came from your Apa's abuela. A mestiza like you, with closer roots to her sangre Indigena. And your coyly hair surely came from the negrita mixed in your blood from your Ama's side everyone tried so hard to erase as they renounced the claim to the third race, all to say they were more Spanish. As if it somehow made them more worthy, of an elevated class. You, who searches in hair straighteners and skin whiteners for a place to call home, have come to the realization that the nostalgia you inherited is from a line of women who have been denied their nature. A line of women who have been shamed and guilted for what their skin color, hair, and curves represented. You can finally see all the beauty that you had been too scared to accept. That your Apa was not lying. That negra, negrita, mi prieta favorita comes from a place of love and that was home the entire time.

Prieta China-China

Corina Villegas | October 2020

Mija

Mi hija

I wish que nunca sufras la humillación

Of being shamed for your womanhood

Que tu sangre, sangre de vida sea honrada

Que nunca tengas que acostumbrarte

To the hands of your uncles, brothers, fathers, and even strangers

Caressing tus piernas, cintura, o cara

Tu forzando una sonrisa para no parecer grosera

While you scream inside with discomfort

Que la maldita tradición de indiferencia

Ya no te force a agachar la mirada

While you give witness

To the maltrato de una de tus hermanas

Mihija

I wish que no tengas que hacer tanto ruido para ser escuchada

That you can be quiet enough to hear your soul calling

Without being taken for weak

I wish que este mundo

No haga mal uso of your nurture, cunning, and intuition

They could create world peace

If only they would let you live long enough to...

Miija

I wish que tu si puedas caminar las calles de tu barrio

Without the fear of being raped, kidnapped, or killed for sport

Que tu si entiendas que el cambio de las malditas tradiciones

Began yesterday pero no termina hoy

Mija is you

I am mija

I wish

Que viva la puta revolución

Que vive dentro de ti y de mi

Hija De La Chingada Coll.

Corina Villegas | October 2020

A tribute to our earth-mother-goddess, creator of life and death, the one with many names: Coatlicue, (she who wore a) serpent skirt, Cihuacoatl, Coatlalopeuh/ Coatlaxopeuh, Guadalupe, La Chingada, La Malinche, La Llorona. She, they, half woman, half snake, in different versions and manifestations, reference our, descendants of the Aztecs- the Mexica people, first mother. The first Mexican woman, mother of Gods and mortals, who would mourn the loss of her children for centuries after their surmised deaths. But we are not all dead. Our ancestors live through us, in us.

Díosa

Me dicen
"I am so glad you're not one of those mujeres caídas"
"Eres una mujer bien hecha y derecha, no como las demás"

But you can keep your manipulative compliments
Hidden-in-honey-and-sugar-objectifications.
I don't want to be your niña buena
Calladita, recatadita, y hasta tu pendejita

A machistas idealization of a woman is her greatest curse
These men and women make arbitrary demands
Based on concepts of divinity
They cannot begin to understand
"Una mujer buena" is unexcused of humanly mistakes

Dicen que la mujer debe de ser calmada como la mar
Pero si la misma mar carga un puto coraje
Que te reventaría los huesos en su tempestad

Dicen que la mujer debe de ser obediente como un perra
Pero ni los perros se quedan donde no son tratados con respeto

Les digo
If you were truly looking for beauty, for goodness, for godliness
You would look into your own Dioses
See they are ever learning, ever expanding
As the universe is
As humans are
If I am a reflection in flesh of those Gods
Diosa I am, human and all
Ever enlightening, ever growing

Learn to have grace with me, not on me
Or don't praise me at all

Unlearning Shame

I am 4 years old
And sweet and innocent
And the world is at my feet
And I love;
I love so much
And I have love for everyone
And my mami has warned me
Against the cruelty of the world
But I could not yet understand
And I try
Yes, I try
And I am timid around new faces
And watchful of strangers
But I could not recognize danger in familiar faces
And I trust him
He said he loves me
He gives me restless attention;
Even plays child games with me
And talks to me
And he tickles me
And invites me into his bedroom
And he begins touching me
And he says to place my hands here
While he places himself there
And reminds me this our secret
And if anyone finds out
Yes, he would be in trouble
And so would I
Now I am his accomplice
And I believe him
I trust him
And I feel sad
And I feel worried
Because I love him
And in some way I want to protect him
And in other way I feel confused
About keeping it from my own mami
Because she has warned me against the cruelty
But she did not say it could also happen
With my papi's younger brother
And my mami recognizes the dullness in my eyes

So she asks if something has happened
She assures me that she could protect me
From ANYONE
And she says mija
"I have noticed you have began wetting the bed again
And some unfamiliar spots in your underwear
You don't smile like you used to
Or go out and play as much
Please do not lie"
And I cry
And I tell her to remember
She had once told me no one was allowed to touch me
Here or there
And I tell her my uncle made me swear
And I do not want to break a promise
And I also do not want to lie
And she says it is okay
No one will be mad
And she asks me one more time
And I tell her that he has touched me
Where no one is allowed
And my mami says okay
And says good night
And the morning comes
And he is gone
And we do not speak
Of him or it again

And I am 13
And my body is changing
And I am quickly learning
About my sexuality
And what I remember of him
Is a foggy nightmare
And I want to forget it
But there is a whisper in my ear
It tells me this body, this flesh is not mine
This whisper has an accent of shame
And it blames me for what has happened
I want to drown out its voice
I bury myself in others

When they ask for loyalty through sex
All i could do is let it happen
I still don't know how to stop it
And it makes me feel empty
And it makes me feel dirty
And some kids judge me
They call me easy
And say I should know better
And I don't know why I do it
And I don't know why I allow it
And they don't know
They don't know I have never said yes
They don't know
I quit loving myself
Long before I could learn how
I reject the flesh of this body
That felt marked by his touch
And I can't take the pain anymore
It begins to numb me
And I want to feel something;
Anything
And I start cutting
And I cut my arms
And I cut my legs
And I cut and cut
Until the blood is flowing
And it is talking
And it is speaking of all the secrets buried within me
And it hurts
And I cry
And cry
Until the flow of my tears
And this dripping blood become One

And I am 18
And still so naïve
And maybe even a little desperate
To redefine my sexuality
With the kind words of a new lover
Because I need love
And have so much love to give
I have met someone
Someone I want to say yes to
And I believe her love will fix me
And this love understands me
And protects me from the outside world
So I give and I give

And I ignore that she takes more than she gives back
And the verbal abuse when she has had one too many drinks
And she says I should judge her only by her sober actions
That's when she says she loves me
But the drunk nights come
Again and again
And the words she slurs could only come from a foe
She says she doesn't remember
So it must not be that bad
And I should be able to handle it
And she asks me to keep it quiet
And I remain silent
Because I know silence is a form of loyalty
I have had enough practice
And in some way I want to protect her
And in another way I just don't want to be alone
But this love drains me
I have not healed
And now I am just more empty
And I am 27
And I am finally learning to reclaim my body
And learning to see all of my shadows as a blessing
And I am realizing that the perversion he planted
Made me a desdichada con dichos de libertad
Set me free from the chains and expectations of society
And I know that purity is not defined by my sexuality
And I know that the submissive female image
Was created by men as a means to control
And I know my body is divinity on earth
And I finally understand that only my own love could heal me
So I welcome the light
AND the darkness within me
I am no longer ashamed
I am no longer guilty
I have learned the power of saying no
Even more so, the power of saying yes
And
Meaning
It

Rebirth

Brown Girl

Refusing invisibility Brown girl

You have reclaimed the curves of your hips

The rizos of your natural hair

The plump of your lips

The thick brownness of your skin

Your chata nose

Your 5'1 -Crowned-

Aztec- Princess-

Big- Headed- Standing- Self

Refusing invisibility Brown girl

You have reclaimed yerba santa

Para limpiarte el Corazón

All your jewels made of gold

The Cortez's on your feet

in some twist of fate

Give homage to the real pinche salvaje

As you stomp on the new conquistador coming for you

The r's that roll off your mouth to trance

The tl's that slither of your split serpent tongue to speak truth

Refusing invisibility Brown girl

You have long claimed the Spanish in your blood

Now you fight for the Indigenous in your soul

Mujer de Color(es)

Corina Villegas / October 2020

A Mujer de Color Anthem

Mujer de Color

Our idealism is more real
Than they allow us to see

We harness the earth
Tierra fuego y agua
Todo en nuestro ser

The fire burns in our hearts
Making ash of those
Who try to stop us

The water flows through our body
Creating new life in the womb
And all that our hands touch

The moon and sun in our soul
Always restoring the balance
Of our earthly incarnation

Where they see devastation
We see renewal

Where they see isolation
We see community

Where they see death
We see rebirth

We are
We are
We are
We are synchronized

Inherent understanding
Everything is connected

Life is a cry-prayer-ceremony

Mujer de Color
We are
The answer
The Manifestation
The source

we are the Gods   to whom they pray

Mujer Grande

I manifest divinity

I am glorious and magical

A galactic legacy

A wielder of fem-in-al energy

I am a Mujer!

One of conviction

A transcending force

Of progressiveness and justice.

I birth new life

In the form of song, flesh, and bark

My fears are subsided

By my desire to see equality prosper

Oh, what a force to be reckoned with

I am a warrior of feminine cunning!

Mothered into resilience

I will not be silenced

A passion burning bright fueled

By my lineage and sisterhood

A full and sagacious manifestation

My voice delivers the verity of my ancestors

A reverberant existence

Handed down from the wake of feminine consciousness

Seraph recipient

I do not shy from my psyche

In my emotional depth you will

Find-meet unassailable strength

You will not question my authority

Not because you are without right

Because the transparency of intention to thrive

Will leave no question in your mind of my truth:

I am grounded and I am a Mujer Grande!

Tortilleras

Jasmine Romero | October 2020

Aside from referring to women who makes tortillas, tortilleras is a common expression, that is typically derogative, used to name or call out homosexual women. It is heavily used in many Latinx cultures with many different speculations of its origins, most deriving from homophobic understandings of homosexuality. As a "Tortilla," I mean to honor both the history of Maiz, which in its own nature is both masculine and feminine, to my culture as well as our liberty to express our sexuality and its orientation as it is most natural to us each. ¡Viva El-La Maíz, Viva El Amor, ¡Viva El Amor Por Maíz!

Ode to Tortillas

Tortillas
Igual que yo
Hijas del maiz
Descendientes de Teōcintli
Gatekeepers of Aztlan
Protectors of my sisters

Oh Tortillas
Nunca nos han desamparado
You have made our company
Through every birria, menudo, y
pozole
Never missed a Noche Buena,
Bautizo, or quinceanera

Tortillas
Tortilleras
Igual que yo
Y Iluminada
Que a través del tiempo
Nos han ensenado
Mejor es la maza
Haiga pan o no haiga

Tortillas
Hechas de mano a mano
Manos de mi madre
Manos de mi abuela
De la vecina
Hasta más allá de la frontera
Son la herencia de amor
De mi sangre y de mi cultura

Tortillas
Nunca nos han desamparado
En tiempo de tristeza
Su maza entre mis dedos
Feels like home
Tu calor sobre el comal
Regresa el fuego a este corazón
Chicano, Americano, siempre Mexicano.

Oh tortillas
Igual que yo
Somos hijas del maíz
Descendientes de Teōcintli
Gatekeepers of Aztlan
Native to these lands

La Vida es un Molcajete

Voy a machacar 15 pétalos de rosas rojas

Para darle sabor de amor a mi vida

Un shot de tequila

Para ser más valiente

Un pinchazo de chile de árbol

Para mantener a mi pasión ardiente

Un poco de leche de los senos de mi amada

Para que nunca se me quite lo mamona

Un puño de yerba santa

Para rechazar a las malas vibras

Un frasco de sueños de ayer y de mañana

Para que siempre pueda hablar con mis ancestros

Ya de camino echarle aguacatito

Para fortalecer a mi pelo chino chino

What's in your Molcajete?

Corina Villegas | October 2020

Pachamama- a- Mama

Madre you are everything

Mi Diosa en tierra ajena

The only God I have ever been able to touch

The bearer of my life

My life-long companion

An ever-giving nurturer

Que me ha permitido vivir de tus frutos

A guest in Your kingdom

You have shown me love and grace

Taught me to honor and respect the life

In you and me

Everything.

Divine Ecstasy

Sweet divine- Impregnate me with the wonder of life

With vibrations that run from my womb to my mind

From my heels to my finger-tips and deep between my thighs

Teach me all the secrets

Of love, balance, and rebirth

Not the resurrection type,

The metamorphosis sub rosa

Never truly beginning,

Never truly ending

Hum them in my ears

Keep whispering them until I cry

Until the floodgates are open

Sweet divine- keep your secrets coming

Cause my third eye to roll back

Make it reach beneath the crevices,

In-betweens, and beyonds

Lead me to the darkness

The place in between space and time

In the stars, the planets, and the moons

In the oceans, rivers, jungles, and woods

 So that I may look into another human's eyes

And bring them into your light

I will show them how to make love to you- Sweet divine.

Prayer for Healing

Creator of life, protectors of the universe

I pray that you heal my mother's wounds

Teach me to heal my own

Allow me to hear my ancestors

For guidance

For redemption

I pray for the wisdom to practice being present

Intentional in all moments of this life

Allow me to create my peace

Find joy in living out my purpose.

The ability to be grateful for the practical

Hone my power to manifest

The courage to choose love, always

The patience to listen before I act

For endless laughter

Tears of pain and joy

I want to feel everything

Never forget I am alive

Know with all of my might

I can always carry on

In this life and after it

In the name of my God and my protectors, I pray.

Acknowledgements

I am so grateful to the Alegria Magazine and Publishing family for helping me create this project. To Davina Ferreira, their founder and CEO, for being a mentor and a voice of inspiration, for opening doors and holding them open for more Latinx writers, like myself, to come through them. For being the first media company to publish my work in The Latinx Poetry Project. You took me in, with the only spec of a vision, and helped me transform it into what it is today: a dream for even greater projects tomorrow.

About the Author

Selena vibes selfie

Aleja Jiménez / April 2020

Alejandra Jimenez

Alejandra Jimenez, otherwise Aleja, is a self-identifying queer chicanx poeta. Aleja is the first-born, of 5 children, of two Mexican- Immigrant parents, from Zacatecas and Jalisco, MX. She grew up in Santa Ana, CA and later in the Inland Empire, epicenters of Latinx communities, as well as frequently visiting her parents' native country, Mexico. Aleja's writing is highly influenced by a desire to become the representation of her people, her culture, and herself she did not see growing up. Living in an undocumented household, Aleja is very familiar with the anxieties caused by the possibility of separation constantly looming, among other everyday struggles faced by immigrant communities. Being part of a family that is primarily made up of women, she has witnessed both, how their growth has been hindered by machista traditions and how they have rebelled against those traditions in their own ways. Like the women that came before her, she aims to use her craft to reclaim her agency and help others, in particular women and femmes, do the same. She moves through the world constantly aware that liberation begins with ourselves and slowly moves into a collective healing. As a declaration of love, Aleja writes from a place of honesty: examining, critiquing, and exposing that which she loves most, in an effort to achieve growth and progress. If Aleja is not reading, writing, or hiking, you can find her bailando through her limpia ceremonies in the comfort of her sacred place, her bedroom.

You can connect with Aleja and more of her Poesía

Via Email: wordsbyalejajimenez@gmail.com
Via Instagram: @wordsbyaleja
Via Website: www.alejajimenez.com

CPSIA information can be obtained
at www.ICGtesting.com
Printed in the USA
BVHW060446261120
593862BV00004B/39

9 781736 149607